Lyrics of Love

Written by: Blaque Diamond

Copyright Page

© 2024 Blaque Diamond

All rights reserved.

No part of this publication may be reproduced, distributed, or transmitted in any form or by any means, including photocopying, recording, or other electronic or mechanical methods, without the prior written permission of the publisher, except in the case of brief quotations embodied in critical reviews and certain other noncommercial uses permitted by copyright law.

For permissions, contact the publisher at diamondintheroughpublications@gmail.com

ISBN: 978-1-7321141-8-0

Table of Contents

Copyright Page ii
About This Book v
Dedication vi
A Mother's Love 1
Broken-Hearted 3
Could This Be? 5
For the Love of God 6
Inner Song 8
Little One 10
Love and War 12
My Kind of Man 14
Love from Within 15
Not Again 17
Nice to Meet You 19
Our God 21
Love on the Beach 23
Questioning 24
Selfish 26
Song of a Mother 27
The Other Woman 30
There's a Difference 31
Torn Between Two 33
Unveiling Ones' Self 35
Wrong Love Blues 37
Unexpected 38
Unconditional 40

Second Chance	42
Prisoner of Love	43
Love Doesn't Hurt	45
Every Beat of My Heart	47
Dream of Self	49
Crush	51
Afterthought	52
Bad Romance	54
A Perfect Love	57
Everyday Love	59
Looking for Love	61
Right Love Wrong Man	63
Self-Love Poem	65
Words of Fire	67
Piece of my Heart	68
If Loving You Is Wrong	70
Broken Promises	71
Fourteen Verses of Love	72
I'll Wait	73
The Love of a Comforter	75
Future Love	77
Clear Bruises	78
Embrace Self	80
Whirlwind	83
Loving You	84
No Boundaries	86
A Forgiving Love	88
About the Author	90
Keep in Contact	91
Other Books by Blaque Diamond	92

About This Book

Love is such a small word, but it has so much meaning. The heart is the centerpiece of every living creature, so we all have the ability to love because love comes from the heart.

This collection of well-crafted poetry explores love in many different forms. From the ups and downs in relationships to delving deep into the importance of self-love. Some poems touch on how God's unconditional love for his children is immeasurable, and how the love of a mother for her child can't be duplicated.

Blaque Diamond explores love in all its dynamics in poetry and verses that allow the reader to envelop themselves in the emotions of love that leave footprints on the heart.

Dedication

This book is dedicated to Amanda Louise Davis-Obigbesan. Thank you for your participation in choosing the title for this collection of love poetry. I love the title you suggested, hence why this book is dedicated to you. Thank you again!

A Mother's Love

This miracle growing inside of me,
Brings joyful tears to my eyes.
I never knew another love like this,
Until the day you came to be.
Your tiny kicks of life,
Reminds me every day that you are mine.
A creation only God could have a hand in,
Is you my son, my baby.
My heart filled with so much love,
It's ready to burst on contact.
When I think of you my child,
I imagine all the things you will do,
And what you can be,
And what you will achieve.
Nothing has ever made me feel this way,
This ever-present inner happiness.
It's all because of you my prince, my heart,
You bring out this side of me.
The day we meet my sweet boy,
Will be the first day of the rest of our lives.
So much we have to learn about one another,
And so much of life we have to experience.
Our bond will be unbreakable,
The hearts of mother and son.
I can't wait to hold you in my arms,
Your sweet essence engulfing my senses.
There are so many plans I have for you,

The world is ours to explore.
These tears I cry are happy ones,
No need for me to feel sad.
I have you forever my love,
And that's a reason to let the rivers flow.
This feeling I feel is all-consuming,
But I don't mind it at all.
I never want to lose this joy,
Because you are the newest love of my life.
No matter what obstacles life may put in our way,
Nothing will get between my love for you.
You are now my highest priority,
The one who will always come first in my life.
These words I write to you come straight from the heart,
This is the result of a mother's unconditional love.

Broken-Hearted

Broken,
Her heart in two.
Excruciating pain,
For a love lost.
Lies and betrayal,
Caused these irregular heartbeats.
The space so hollow,
Caving in her chest.
Emptiness,
Has her crying out from within.
Tears of pain,
Trails rivers down her face.
Why does love hurt so much?
Why to her?
When all she wanted is to love,
And be loved.
A dismal world,
She sees throughs clouded vision.
Blurred by her many tears cried,
For a broken love.
Unforgiving,
Her heart needs time.
To mend and heal,
To bring back the laughter.

Anger and disappointment,
Have her thinking the worst.
That she isn't meant to be loved,
By anyone.
Or everything she should love,
Is pain and incompleteness.
This hurt shall pass,
And she will love again.
The pieces of her broken heart,
Will be fixed.
The sorrow no more,
Tears of happiness will replace.
The trails of pain,
Will be no more.
She will no longer be,
A broken-hearted woman.

Could This Be?

Could this be what I've always hoped for?
On my knees at night praying,
Asking God to send down to me,
A love of my own.
Could this really be?
The long awaited answer to my prayers?
My chance to finally find happiness,
Standing right here in front of me.
Could this truly be happening?
Something so pure and precious,
Leaves me wondering about the future.
Are we destined to be?
Together in love forever?
My knight and shining armor,
Here to save this damsel in distress.
Could this be the time?
The time I've waited so patiently for?
My heart believes this is it,
At long last it's my turn.
Love has visited me again,
It has granted me another opportunity.
A chance at forever with you,
I will embrace it,
Hold on to it tightly,
Never letting it go.
Could this be real?

For the Love of God

Oh, seeker of truth, open your heart wide,
Embrace the divine love, let it be your guide.
For in loving God, a boundless embrace,
We find tranquility, in this tumultuous place.

When tribulations rage and trials befall,
God's love transcends, embracing one and all.
Through heartache and sorrow, He'll hold you near,
A refuge in pain, erasing all fear.

For in loving God, our hearts they align,
The divine presence, serene and sublime.
In His love, we find purpose and strength,
Benevolence and kindness, extending the lengths.

With every step taken on this earthly terrain,
Loving God's grace helps us to sustain.
His teachings a compass, guiding us right,
To live a life virtuous, pure, and bright.

In adoration of God, joy blossoms entwined,
A love eternal, in His presence, we find.
Beyond earthly desires, our souls touch the sky,
A sense of belonging, as our spirits soar high.

From dawn's first light to each twilight's end,
God's love reigns supreme, a faithful friend.
Countless blessings bestowed, every breath we take,
A testament of love, more than words can make.

Through prayer and reflection, we reach the core,
A connection with God, forevermore.
Within our souls, His love does repose,
A divine union, where eternal peace flows.

Inner Song

In the tender morn of my soul's awakening,
I wandered through meadows of unrequited love,
Where roses wore thorns, and doves soared away,
Leaving me yearning, with a heart dreaming of.

Yet amidst the shadows, a flicker did ignite,
An ember of resilience, burning bright,
For in my solitude, I found endless grace,
In the depths of my being - my sacred space.

I, a tempestuous storm, craving validation,
But now, I embark on an inward exploration,
For within lies a galaxy of self-worth untold,
A universe of love, waiting to unfold.

No longer shall I seek approval or rhyme,
For my inner song is harmonious and sublime,
In the mirror's reflection, my gaze shall find,
A soul ablaze with self-love, courage, and kind.

Like a phoenix, I rise from the ashes of despair,
Embracing my flaws, for they make me rare,
And the scars etched upon me, like rivers that flow,
Remind me, in strength, I shall forever grow.

Gone are the days of relying on another's glance,
I, alone, hold the key to my joyful dance,
For it is through self-acceptance I truly thrive,
Like a soaring bird, forever alive.

I shall bathe in self-care, a sanctuary sweet,
As I nourish my heart, with love replete,
The universe within, an eternal embrace,
A symphony of self-worth, a hymn of grace.

No longer do I seek love's barren coast,
For my soul abounds with a love that's most,
A love that needs no validation to bloom,
But thrives within, dispelling all gloom.

So let the world whisper and tell me not,
Of the love I lack, for I have sought,
Within myself, a river pure and deep,
A love that's mine, mine alone, to keep.

Oh, my spirit, rise high, like the moon above,
Embrace your worth, a testament of self-love,
For in the absence of unrequited affection,
I shall bask in the glory of self-reflection.

Now, I stand tall, a beacon of self-discovery,
Embracing the beauty of this love, unequivocally,
For in the absence of external validation,
I find solace and strength in self-dedication.

So, let the winds carry away love's lament,
For my heart is content, self-love, my ascent,
With resilience as my armor, and self-acceptance my art,
I am a masterpiece of love, forged within my own heart.

Little One

I haven't met you yet, but I love you already,
To be your mother, I'm nervous and scared, but I'm ready.
A pretty little girl or a handsome little boy,
You haven't arrived yet, but you're already my pride and joy.
I just have so much of my love to give to you,
Will your favorite color be pink, or will it be blue?
You are a blessing from God that I will always appreciate,
To have you in my life, nine months is too long to wait.
I want to cradle you in my arms and shower you with love,
Because you are a precious gift from my lord above.
A beautiful little girl who looks just like me,
A handsome little man you will grow up to be.
Ten perfect fingers and ten little toes,
Beautiful brown eyes and a cute button nose.
Tears fill my eyes when I think of you,
There are so many wonderful plans I have for me and you.
You're my new purpose in life; you're the beat of my heart,
Nothing and no one will ever tear us apart.

*I vow to be the best mommy to you that I can be,
My purpose is to show you that my love will last for eternity.
You have the key to my heart, and you don't even know it yet,
How you came to be, I have no regrets.
Sometimes things in life just happen for a reason,
Because life is something we have no guarantees in.
I pray for you my child each and every day,
Wondering what will be the first words you say.
There is so much we have to learn about each other,
You my child, and me your mother.
I want to give you the kind of life I never had,
I want your days to be full of joy and happiness, not sad.
It makes me smile to know that I have someone else to live for,
I don't have to wonder what true love is anymore.
It's not hard to answer the question why,
Every time I think of you, I start to cry.
It's the love I feel for you deep inside my heart,
That makes my emotional waterworks start.
I'm anxiously anticipating the day I get to meet you,
So, you can know that you're my heart, and how much mommy loves you.*

Love and War

We are constantly going back and forth,
My heart plummets south, then travels back north.
When your lips touch mine, you set me on fire,
As I look into your eyes; all I see is desire.
We go full-circle, around and around,
Straight up, then right back down.
What we have together, no one else can touch,
The years we've been together explain our love so much.
It's all my fault, then it's all yours,
As we angrily slam the bedroom doors.
You're the king of the palace, and I'm the crowned queen,
Soft music and candles are what sets our love scene.
This love is like a fast-moving roller coaster,
Like a crazy ride on an amusement park poster.
Holding hands lovingly as we stroll through the park,
Tattooing each other's name, leaving a permanent mark.
Sometimes you're hot, and sometimes I'm cold,
It's unclear sometimes if we should hold on or fold.
Your love constantly keeps me on an all-time high,
I'm floating so high; I can literally touch the sky.
The tears streaming down my face display my pain,
This last harsh fight is going to leave an ugly stain.
This love is genuine, and we're happy to be together,
We've promised to love and trust each other forever.

*Sometimes I can't stand you, and you get on my nerves,
When we're in the midst of an argument you spew angry words.
Flowers and candies aren't as sweet as your kisses,
That's why I'm proud that you're my Mr. and that I'm your misses.
I just want to walk away when the waters get tough,
You angrily shout you're fed up, and you've had enough.
A love like this could never really be that bad,
You've given me the best memories I've ever had.
Shattered pictures and wine glasses litter the floor,
My throat is so sore; I can't yell anymore.
The two halves of our heart make us a perfect whole,
To make this love last forever is our lifetime goal.
Sometimes you're cold, and sometimes I'm hot,
Love and war all twisted together in knots.
The love we have for each other shines brightly through our eyes,
We greet each other with smiles each morning when we rise.
I know everything in a relationship won't fit together perfectly,
But I'm perfect for you, and you for me.
First, it's love, then it's war,
Do we really know what we're even fighting for?
Despite the ups and downs, we know our love is true,
At the end of the day, all that matters is I love you.*

My Kind of Man

He is proud to claim me as his woman,
Making me smile is his pride and his joy.
When I knock on his heart, he lets me in,
He is a grown man, not a little boy.
He is not afraid to express himself,
Coming home to him each day is a treat.
I am what he wants, not anyone else,
His sweet kisses turn up my body heat.
When the road gets bumpy, he smooth's it out,
Handsome and charismatic, that he is.
He is confident in himself, no doubt,
I love that sexy baritone of his.
He believes in building a long-lasting foundation.
His kind of love needs no explanation.

Love from Within

In this world of constant confusion and haste,
Where self-doubt lingers like an unwelcome guest,
It is vital to unlock your heart's precious gate,
And let self-love bloom, your soul to infest.

For how can you travel life's steep, treacherous climbs,
Without the light of self-love guiding your way?
It is the beacon that shines through the darkest of times,
Nurturing your spirit, allowing it to sway.

Loving yourself is not vanity, but a necessity,
A testament to your worth, a celebration of existence.
You are deserving of affection, unabashedly,
So, kindle that flame within, let it dance with persistence.

Embrace your imperfections, for they make you whole,
For no rose is without its delicate thorns.
Adorn your flaws proudly, let them be your soul's console,
For they tell a tale of resilience, beautifully reborn.

See each scar etched upon your heart as a trophy,
A testament of battles won; fears conquered.

They show the world that you are not defined by your apology,
But by the love within, fiercely undeterred.

Remember, in the realm of self-love, you are the master,
You have the power to banish self-doubt and despair.
Accept yourself as you are, a divine disaster,
For love starts within, an endless affair.

When you love yourself, you radiate like the morning sun,
Illuminating the lives around you, a force to admire.
Your love becomes a gift, cherished by everyone,
Spreading warmth and joy, rousing hearts from slumber.

So go forth, dear soul, and marvel at your worth,
With each step, whisper sweet nothings to your reflection.
For self-love is the key to unlocking life's true mirth,
Embrace its magic and cherish your own affection.

In this journey of life, let self-love be your guide,
A compass that directs you towards happiness and bliss.
For when you love yourself, you'll realize with pride,
That the importance of self-love is simply in this.

Not Again

Oh no, not this same shit again,
Why do I keep falling for these types of men?
Broken promises and constant conflicting lies,
Deep feelings of love slowly turn into despise.
Control, domination, and abuse is the goal,
Why not love me honestly with your heart and soul?
Gentle hugs and passionate kisses are all I crave,
Your harsh words and actions are completely depraved.
You try to use my faith as a form of manipulation,
Me trembling in fear brings you immense pleasure and elation.
Punching fists and kicking feet is your version of love,
I'm cowering on the floor as you hover above.
What happened to the happy life you promised me?
Oh, it was all just a well-scripted fantasy.
At first, everything was perfect, royal, and divine,
But all that changed once I signed on the dotted line.
Your mask came off; your true intentions were revealed,
The moment I let you in, my fate was sealed.
Do I wish I had kept it moving when you reached out?
Yes, because then I wouldn't have another bad romance to write about.
Is it so hard to find someone whose love is really true?

Someone's personality flaws that are far between and few.
Toxicity and negativity are all I seem to find,
Bad habits, insecurities, and unstable states of mind.
You've got mommy issues, so a woman is your punching bag,
You're such a great magician that you hid all the red flags.
How was I supposed to know that I'd been duped once again?
By all of these little boys perpetrating to be real men.
You can't get your way, so your fist does the talking,
I know my worth and what i deserve, so my feet do the walking.
I won't stand by while you attempt to degrade and tear me down,
I'm a beautiful queen; upon my head is my diamond crown.
What doesn't kill me only makes me that much stronger,
To fear for my life; I have to no longer.
Just another story of survival I share with the world,
But I swear I'm not someone's broken-hearted little girl.
Oh no, it won't be this same shit again,
Because I won't be falling for anymore of these kinds of men.

Nice to Meet You

Our hands brush as we walk by each other,
My heart begins to flutter.
For this stranger I don't know why,
I just feel the urge to cry.
Have I met you somewhere before?
Maybe you opened my door.
You turn back to gaze at me puzzled,
Your expression befuddled.
The smile you give is confused but curious,
I am starting to think that maybe I am delirious.
I ask your name,
And to my surprise, it's the same.
As someone I used to know.
We sit down to chat,
And imagine that!
We like most of the same things,
My ears start to ring.
Again, I ask you if you're sure,
That we have never met before?
And you say to me,
In another lifetime, maybe?
This person I used to know,
I loved him so.
We could talk about anything,
We did everything.

We shared so much,
Our hopes,
Our dreams,
Our trust.
You don't look like him,
But you remind me so much of him.
In a strange way,
Maybe you are a reincarnation,
Or maybe just my imagination.
Am I crazy?
Or just maybe?
You are my lost love,
Sent to me from above.
There is just this indescribable connection,
This heart-pounding affection.
This feeling I feel is true,
For some strange reason, I think I love you.
Nice to meet you.

Our God

The pains of your life won't last always,
The glorious work of our God is sure to amaze.
He doesn't burden you with more than you can carry,
Even when your mind, body, and soul are wary.
Lift up his name and give him praise,
He's responsible for bringing better days.
Don't doubt his love or the miracles he works,
Being a child of God is such an honorable perk.
Get on your knees and pray; he hears your plea,
Just have faith in his soul-cleansing words and you will see.
What doesn't kill you only makes you stronger,
To find the peace you seek, you have to search no longer.
God has the answers to all your questions,
Go to him first, I have no other suggestions.
He is a comforter, redeemer, and a spiritual healer,
When you know our God, his love's like an invisible concealer.
Just call out his name, and he will always be there,
No matter how near or far, he's everywhere.
His love is unconditional and has no limits,
To speak to him doesn't take long, just a few minutes.

*You ought to know the awesome and merciful God we serve,
To give him all the praise and glory is what he deserves.
Our God, our God, our wonderful God,
Loves his children greatly although we are flawed.
Thank him for his many blessings each and every day,
He has the power to dry all your tears away.
There's no God greater than the man above,
There's no one who can show us a greater love.
The fact we worship his name isn't weird or odd,
Because he is worthy. Our God, our God. Our mighty God!*

Love on the Beach

Walking together on the sun-bleached sand,
The gentle waves crashed against the shore.
Wrapped in our own little world hand in hand.
As the fishes dance on the ocean floor.
Seagulls flying high against the blue sky.
Let's enjoy a beach picnic just for two.
Lost in each other's space just you and I,
Feeding each other the way lovers do.
Playing some music to set the mood right,
Talking and laughing as the day goes by.
We can stay all day until the moonlight.
On our blankets of divine love, we lie.
A beautiful day of pure love this is,
As we end our day with a few kisses.

Questioning

Is his love for me true?
Does he mean it when he says, I love you?
Is he playing games with my heart?
Just playing a role; doing his part?
Should I believe his eyes?
Do they tell me lies?
His words were so sweet,
Dripping with desire, or is it deceit?
I want to believe in romance,
I want to give love another chance.
But at what cost?
Isn't there so much I've already lost?
I don't want to play the fool,
This game of love can be so cruel.
Can I trust that he won't hurt me?
Will he love and cherish me the way I should be?
My heart wants to give love another try,
But will he break my heart and make me cry?
Everything that glitters isn't gold,
If I should love him or not, I haven't been sold.
Should I give him my loyalty and trust?
Will he just take it and bury it in the dust?
Or will he take it and hold it close to his chest?
His desire is to show me nothing but the best.

Is he strong enough to mend my broken heart?
Am I willing to experience a new start?
I'm so confused; I don't know what to do,
Which way I should go; I don't have a clue.
Will he do all that he swears?
Is he able to wipe away all my tears?
How do you take a chance when you've been hurt before?
I don't want my heart to hurt anymore.
He promises to be the man I need him to be,
But will he be able to do that successfully?
I'm questioning, questioning, and second-guessing,
Will his love be a curse, or a magnificent blessing?

Selfish

Do you love yourself?
Enough to get out of a bad relationship.
Do you love yourself?
Enough to take care of your mental health.
Do you love yourself?
Enough to invest in your growth and personal development.
Do you love yourself?
Enough to fix the broken parts of you.
Do you love yourself?
Enough to go after your dreams and goals.
Do you love yourself?
Enough to say no when the situation calls for it.
Do you love yourself?
Enough to learn from your past mistakes
Do you love yourself?
Enough to take care of your physical and spiritual body.
Do you love yourself?
Enough not to lose yourself in others
Do you love yourself?
Enough to know that thinking about self doesn't make you selfish.

Song of a Mother

In the quiet hush of twilight,
beneath the sleepy stars,
a mother cradles her young child,
a love that knows no bounds.

Her arms, a shelter from the world,
wrapping tenderly around,
the fragile innocence that rests,
in the warmth of her embrace.

Soft whispers fill the gentle air,
like feathers on a breeze,
as she sings a lullaby,
that echoes through the night.

Her voice, a symphony of love,
that dances through the air,
a melody to calm the storms,
that rage within his soul.

With each sweet note that she sings,
a love song from the heart,
she weaves a kaleidoscope of dreams,
and tenderness imparts.

She strokes his tiny curly head,
with hands so soft and kind,

a touch that speaks of magic,
of love that's unconfined.

Her touch, a soothing balm of love,
a ripple in life's tide,
it heals his scrapes and bruises,
as she cradles him inside.

Through the joys and challenges,
of each day that they will face,
she champions his every step,
a guide through time and space.

She is his compass in the storm,
a beacon in the dark,
leading him to shores unknown,
with faith her lantern sparks.

And as he grows and ventures out,
the mother's heart still swells,
with love and unending pride,
for all she's loved, and loveliness beheld.

For in her child, a reflection,
of all that she holds dear,
her dream and her legacy,
forever drawing near.

Oh, the bond between a mother and child,
a love that knows no end,
a tapestry of memories,
that only they can mend.

In this sacred dance of life,
hand-in-hand they'll go,
forever bound together,
in a love that overflows.

The Other Woman

Giving yourself to someone else's man,

Putting all your time into pleasing him.

Leaving her is not in his future plan,

If you think he loves you; you are so dim.

Slashing his tires won't do a damn thing,

Harassing his wife won't make him want you.

Faking a baby won't get you a ring,

Stocking him won't make him change his mind boo.

Pleading with him to just give you a chance,

He has told you that this thing has to end.

This ain't no ordinary romance,

Your broken heart you hope he will soon mend.

No matter how dirty you try to fight,

In the end, you will never be his wife.

There's a Difference

The phrase, "I love you" is so frequently used,
Often even abused,
But so many people have it confused.
Just because you care for someone,
Doesn't mean that in love will be the outcome.
There is a difference between being in love,
And having love.
Love is a word used so loosely,
People claim it so profusely.
I wonder if they really know the meaning,
Head over heels they find themselves careening.
Into the pot of mixed emotions,
With misconceived notions.
I can love you,
But not be in love with you too.
Being in love is different,
But having love doesn't mean your feelings are insignificant.
You can love someone without being in love with them,
Love is something that should be cherished like a rare gem.
Having a love for someone means you care for the person,
The feelings in your heart are like a small insertion.

Being in love means your whole heart is in it,
To lose the one you love leaves your being like a vast empty pit.
Having love for someone can just be appreciation,
A formation of feelings,
That sometimes confuse the situation.
Just because you have love for a person, doesn't mean that you're in love,
It's just your heart they have a piece of.
I love you,
How do you know you really do?
Do I have love for you, or am I in love with you?
There's a difference you see,
That's the key.
Do you love me?
Or do you just have love for me?
Is the question that needs to be asked,
Your true feelings unmasked,
Will it last?
SO please don't be confused.
Or abuse the phrase, "I love you",
Which is so frequently used.

Torn Between Two

I don't know how this happened, and I can't figure out when,
But I find myself in love with two different men.
One has my heart, and the other has my mind,
Have you ever heard of a sticky situation of this kind?
They're both good to me, but one treats me better,
With flowers and candy and sweet love letters.
Long walks in the park and candle-light dinners,
How can I choose? In my eyes, they're both winners.
One likes basketball, and the other likes soccer,
One is shy, and the other is a talker.
How did I get myself into this sticky situation?
Having two men can cause drama and frustration.
How can I choose which of them I love the most?
When one cooks me chicken, and the other cooks me roast.
I've tried and tried to pick one out of the two,
But when it comes to love, that's so hard to do.
Having two different men has its hurdles and challenges,
I just hope my decision won't cause ever-lasting damages.

One lives in the country, and the other in the city,
The fact that I can't choose between the two is such a pity.
Trips around the world on exotic vacations,
I met one on the train and the other at the bus station.
It may seem quite selfish for me to have two men,
One named Joey and the other named Ken.
If this thing called love wasn't so difficult and confusing,
Then I wouldn't have this complicated task of choosing.
In my heart and mind, I feel I should have them both,
Because with time with each I see expansion and growth,
One is a lawyer and the other is a judge,
Ken craves vanilla and Joey loves fudge.
Help me, help me, I need to make a decision,
My heart and mind are heading for a drama-filled collision.
I can't believe that I'm torn between two lovers,
But the craziest thing about it all is that they're twin brothers.

Unveiling Ones' Self

In this tapestry of life, where stories intertwine,
Dare to remove the mask, let your true self brightly shine.
For in one's vulnerability, strength can truly be found,
Unveiling the many layers, to a world that astounds.
So read me a poem adorned with your truth,
Where vulnerability reigns, empowering our youth.
Let us venture into the depths previously unseen,
Embracing the beauty in revealing what won't demean.
In vulnerability, walls begin to crumble,
As we share our struggles, fears, and stumble.
Those who meet us in these empathetic and tender spaces,
Breathe compassion, offering warm embraces.
So read me a poem adorned with your truth,
Where vulnerability reigns, empowering our youth.
Let us venture into the depths previously unseen,
Embracing the beauty in revealing what won't demean.
Oh, vulnerability, the gateway to connection,
A catalyst for the soul's deepest affection.
The walls we build hinder intimacy's flight,
Yet vulnerability helps forge connections, bright.

In unveiling our struggles, masked by a smile,
We find solace in others, understanding all the while.
For strength lies in the courage to reveal our core,
And empathy blossoms, creating a bond forevermore.
So read me a poem adorned with your truth,
Where vulnerability reigns, empowering our youth.
Let us venture into the depths previously unseen,
Embracing the beauty in revealing what won't demean.

Wrong Love Blues

Once again, I'm singing this song,
Once again, I'm singing this song,
About another love gone wrong.

I tried this love thing once again,
I tried this love thing once again,
I keep falling for the wrong kind of men.

Just when I think I've got it right,
Just when I think I've got it right,
Here he comes just wanting to fight.

Constant lies and toxic behaviors,
Constant lies and toxic behaviors,
The daily stress is doing me no favors.

I need to get myself out of here,
I need to get myself out of here,
Have to be strong and show no fear.

I want someone who won't abuse,
I want someone who won't abuse,
Don't want to keep singing the wrong love blues.

Unexpected

This thing I'm feeling comes as such a surprise,
I feel like I have a new smile and sparkle in my eyes.
I think of only you each morning when I rise,
No matter how hard I try, I can't disguise.

The way I feel about you I can't explain,
Thoughts and memories of you are always on my brain.
These feelings are good I can't complain,
I just hope my feelings won't be in vain.

No one could've told me I would fall for you,
Because this is not something I normally do.
They say love can be right in front of you; well, I guess that's true,
Because before meeting you I didn't have a clue.

That a man such as yourself could even exist,
So far you have all A's on my checklist.
I am so curious; I can't resist,
Wanting to know what it will be like when we first kiss.

I definitely did not go looking for love,
I guess fate had its own plans, sort of,
Someone was working their own magic above,
I want to know what it is like to be truly loved.

I have been hurt and disappointed in love in my past,
My heart broken into pieces and even smashed.
I don't know what is in our future forecast,
But I hope it is the love I have been searching for at long last.

These feelings are different; these feelings are new.
So, I hope your feelings are solid; I hope they are true.
This may be a lot to swallow or even to chew,
But I think I am falling in love with you.

Unconditional

Oh, God's love, so vast and deep,
Embracing us, even in times when we may stumble or weep.
Unconditional, like a river flowing endlessly,
In this love, we find solace and tranquility.

In the vastness of existence, where stars shine above,
God's love shines brightest, unconditional and pure as a dove.
A love that knows no boundaries, no reason to define,
Embracing every soul, tender and divine.

Through life's stormy seas and trials, we face,
God's love remains steadfast, a never-faltering embrace.
When darkness veils our hearts, and hope seems far away,
God's love lights our path, leading us back today.

In times of despair and shattered dreams,
God's love surrounds us, stitching up the seams.
An unwavering presence, a shoulder to lean,
God's love is ever-present, an eternal gleam.

When we feel unworthy, burdened by guilt and shame,
God's love whispers gently, erasing all blame.
It lifts us from the darkness, bringing light into our soul,
A love that heals, makes us whole.

Oh, God's love, so vast and deep,
Embracing us, even in times when we may stumble or weep.
Unconditional, like a river flowing endlessly,
In this love, we find solace and tranquility.

Second Chance

If only I could have the chance,
Another opportunity,
To do things over again,
I would take it with no hesitation.
A chance to make things right with you,
A chance to take back the angry words,
That we rained upon each other's hearts.
What was said wasn't really meant,
It was just the anger talking.
If I could have a chance,
To redo the hands of time.
A chance to get back our spine-tingling love,
A chance to rekindle the flames,
A chance to get things back,
To the way it is supposed to be.
Another opportunity to recreate the magic we used to share.
All I need is another chance,
To be with you again.
We can right the wrongs,
Wipe away all the tears.
We can get the old thing back,
It is going to take some time.
But all we need,
Is that second chance.

Prisoner of Love

My heart wants exactly what it wants,
Beating rapidly is my heart's response.
I never want to lose this beautiful feeling,
It's my hopelessly imprisoned love you are stealing.
Being shackled to you is something I don't mind,
Another love like this I won't ever find.
Cuffed together as eternal prisoners,
This kind of love needs no weekly visitors.
Locked behind our invisible bars,
Our words of love carved like permanent scars.
The bail to escape this love is denied,
You wouldn't be able to break out even if you tried.
We're caged together like two love birds,
Our only conversation is the sound of our sweet words.
We don't need food; we can survive off love alone,
The next time we will see the daylight to us is unknown.
The guards know they can't break this love up,
To get through to our hearts can't be done with back up.
The judge can throw the entire book at us,
And I promise you that we won't make a single fuss.
We don't mind that our love is locked down,
Because when we are together our love is always around.

There's no need for fancy expensive lawyers,
We're guilty as charged, so command your orders.
There is no probation or early release date,
I don't want anyone else as my love mate.
I'd rather we stay in our love cell together,
With a love like this we can make it through whatever.
My heart is jailed, and yours is too,
There is no other I'd do my time with than you.

Love Doesn't Hurt

You say this is love,
But love doesn't hurt.
I shouldn't feel this way,
So sad and confused.
Aren't we supposed to be happy?
Then why am I crying?
These tears of pain,
Stream rivers down my face.
My heart is broken,
In pieces scattered all around.
I want to stay and fight,
But I also want to give up.
Those angry words,
And slaps to my face.
Don't symbolize love to me,
They aren't tenderness,
I shouldn't have to flinch from your touch.
Too afraid to utter a word,
Things aren't supposed to be this way.
I'm sure this isn't what love is,
Why do you treat me this way?
I thought our love would last forever,
This pain brings me to my knees.
My hands folded in prayer,
Asking God to change your ways.

And bring peace to my life,
I can't live like this.
This is too much to bare,
I want the fairytale.
The magic of what love is supposed to be.
My pillow was drenched in my tears.
The rhythm of my heart is off-balanced.
This can't be love.
It can't really be this bad.
This physical and emotional pain.
Has taken over my life.
I'm so unhappy.
Life has no meaning for me.
I know in my heart.
That this isn't love.
But why do I stay?
Continue to endure your harsh treatment.
That's the question I ask myself.
But I still don't have an answer.
This can't be right.
This definitely isn't love.
Because love is kind.
Love is sweet.
Love is gentle.
And I know love shouldn't hurt.

Every Beat of My Heart

Yes, you are my sweet boy.
Every beat of my heart.
You bring me so much joy,
When I wake up to you each day.
And see your handsome face,
You melt all my fears away.
We are so blessed to have one another,
No one will ever take your place.
You my son, and me your mother,
My world has been changed for the better.
Nothing about your existence is wrong,
That's why I write you these letters.
My heart swells with so much pride,
To know that you belong to me.
And I will never leave your side,
I will always give you all of me.
Never just a piece,
But all that I am, and what I can be.
Everything I do is for you,
Nothing but the best for my prince.
Because that is what mothers are supposed to do.
There is no other way,
For me to say how you make me feel.
Because it's more than just the words I say,
Thoughts of you constantly fill my mind.

Giving me the strength to keep pushing on each day.
This kind of love is hard to find,
Every beat of my heart.
Pumps my love for you,
No one will ever tear us apart.
We have each other always and forever,
Summer, fall, winter, and spring.
No matter what happens later; we will always be together,
Watching you grow and learn each day,
Fills my heart with happiness.
I love the silly songs we sing and the fun games we play,
These happy tears I cry are for,
The many plans I have for us,
I don't think I could ever love someone more.
My love for you stretches from here to beyond,
There is no glue that is stronger,
Than the strength of our special bond.
There is much of the world we can explore together,
We're making vacation plans for the future.
To ensure you have the best childhood memories ever,
Seven lovely months so far, but it's just a start,
We have so much more time left.
Because you are every beat of my heart.

Dream of Self

In dream's embrace, a world anew unfolds,
Where passions bloom, and daring tales are told.
For dreams, like rivers, carve paths through weary hearts,
And lend us strength to face life's daunting charts.

In this symphony, where souls take flight,
Self-love unfurls its wings, the beacon of light.
Where doubts are silenced, and fears are laid to rest,
For dreams ignite the fire within our chest.

With pen in hand, or brush upon canvas wide,
We wander through the realms where greatness resides.
The dreams we nurture, like tender saplings, grow,
As we water them with passion and let them sow.

They paint our skies with hues of whispered hope,
And lend us wings on which our spirits cope.
For self-love weaves the tapestry of might,
Allowing dreams to take flight, in shadowed night.

Imagine, then, a garden of resolute dreams,
Where vivid sunflowers dance and moonlit rivers gleam.

Each petal grafts resilience in our core,
As self-love flows, a current to explore.

In silence, we can hear the whispers of our dreams,
As stars align to guide our chosen schemes.
For dreams, like constellations, map the way,
To self-fulfillment and a brighter day.

So, seize the reins, and with conviction stride,
Through valleys deep, and mountains tall, with pride.
For dreams shall gift you strength through the darkest night,
And open doors to realms of pure delight.

Embrace the challenges that lie ahead,
For dreams, like seeds, are nurtured when they're fed.
With determination as our guiding star,
We'll chase our dreams and triumph from afar.

So, let us celebrate the power we hold,
To carve our destinies, truth be told.
For in the pursuit of dreams, we learn to soar,
And find the love within us, evermore.

Crush

I can't believe I have a silly school-girl crush,

Every time I hear his name it makes me blush.

My heart starts fluttering, and my palms get sweaty,

My stomach does backflips, and my legs feel like spaghetti.

How can such a man have me feeling this way?

He's constantly on my mind each and every day.

I smell his manly fragrance wafting through the air,

I can imagine running my fingers through his curly hair.

When we're together he lights up my world,

He's my man, and I'm his girl.

This isn't like me; this is quite unusual,

The best thing of all is the feelings are mutual.

Afterthought

You say you love me,
But why am I always an afterthought?
I'm not a priority in your life,
Only last on your list.
I try to tell you how I feel,
But it does no good.
You don't understand,
Or you just don't care at all.
Why say those words then?
Love requires action.
When I cry at night,
You aren't there to wipe away the tears.
The sadness that you caused,
Because I'm an afterthought.
Everyone else comes before me,
But you want me as your spouse?
I'm not going to beg for your time,
Why should I?
You say you care,
But your actions show me different.
My wants fall on deaf ears,
You don't hear my pain.
I'm not asking for much,
So, I don't understand why it's so hard.

Maybe you're being pulled in too many directions,
This is much more than you can handle.
A relationship is not for you,
Because you can't prioritize.
But you just don't get it,
I don't think you ever will.
You wouldn't treat me this way,
If I wasn't an afterthought.
My heart breaks in two,
Every time I call, and you aren't here.
Everyone else can count on you,
But sadly; I can't.
When I need you the most,
You're never around.
On bended knees you profess your love,
But where do I fit in?
You're always too busy,
Quality time is a distant memory.
On important occasions,
I find myself left alone.
What will it take?
For you to see me; and see what you're doing to me.
If I was a priority in your life,
Then I wouldn't be an afterthought.

Bad Romance

She thought he was her superman,
Superman he was not.
Not at all,
All he was.
Was a devil in disguise,
Disguised were his true intentions.
Intending to hurt her,
Her life is in his hands.
Hands that belong to him,
Him who takes advantage.
Advantages in this relationship there is none,
None of the whispered promises.
Promises to be good to her.
Her heart wanted to believe,
Believe he would keep his words.
Words of love,
Love didn't live there.
There was nothing but pain,
Pain to her heart and body.
Body covered in bruises,
Bruised is her heart.
Heart smashed and broken,
Broken is her spirit.

Spirit of her dreams,
Dreams long forgotten.
Forgotten is her smile,
Smiling doesn't exist.
Existence is a burden,
Burdens weigh down her mind.
Mind full of crazy thoughts,
Thoughts that could land her in jail.
Jail is no place for her,
Her heart is trapped.
Trapped in this dangerous situation,
Situation she can't seem to get out.
Out is all she wants,
Wanted someone to love.
Love he pretended,
Pretended he did.
Did he really love her?
Her love was true.
True was not his feelings,
Feelings of power.
Power over her life,
Life has no meaning.
Meaning she must escape,
Escape from her hell.

Hell, she is living in,
In an effort to save her life.
Life she wants to live,
Live in happiness.
Happiness is all she's ever wanted.
Wanted to be truly loved,
Loved the way she dreamed.
Dream she plans to fulfill,
Fulfill her heart's desire.
Desire to be loved,
Loved by the right one.
One who will not hurt her,
Her heart will heal.
Heal from the pain,
Pain will no longer take over.
Over will be the torment,
Torment of a bad romance.

A Perfect Love

In the depths of the boundless universe,
Where stars dance in ethereal grace,
There exists a love that defies reason,
A love that knows no end, no boundary.

God's love, a tapestry woven in radiant hues,
Embraces imperfect people on Earth,
A love that cradles and holds them close,
With gentle arms that whisper solace.

In this vast expanse of divine affection,
Flaws and imperfections lose their shackles,
For God's love is a mirror that reflects,
The true beauty hidden within each soul.

Like a compassionate river, it flows,
Through the valleys of despair and doubt,
Softly murmuring melodies of hope,
To awaken dormant dreams in weary hearts.

In God's love, each person finds solace,
For it knows no judgment, no condemnation,
Only acceptance, unyielding and profound,
A sanctuary for the burdened spirit to rest.

It is the lighthouse guiding the lost,
A beacon of light in the darkest night,
For God's love transcends human understanding,
Illuminating even the deepest abyss of pain.

In this boundless love, we find strength,
To rise above our own self-doubt,
For it is a love that nurtures growth,
And encourages our souls to blossom and thrive.

Like a benevolent gardener tending to fragile blooms,
God's love cultivates seeds of compassion,
Nurturing kindness and understanding,
Watering the roots of unity and empathy.

And so, let us revel in this divine love,
Let us bask in its warmth and grace,
For it has the power to heal wounded hearts,
And ignite the fire of hope in weary souls.

Let this love be our refuge and our guide,
A constant reminder of our inherent worth,
For we are imperfect people, embraced by grace,
In the profound depths of God's unwavering love.

Everyday Love

Our love is not celebrated just once a year,
There is no guess work; our feelings are clear.
We celebrate our love each and every day,
By the things we do, and by the things we say.

Gifts and flowers are special treats,
But our communication is the sweetest of sweets.
Let's go out; let's enjoy the night,
Then when we get back, we can get each other right.

Our love creates its very own music,
Shot in the heart with the arrows of cupid.
Sometimes things are done, and sometimes things are said,
But we cannot be angry with each other before going to bed.

Quality time is a relationship must,
We can't be complete without loyalty and trust.
You've locked down my heart; you have the key,
Even though sometimes we may disagree.

Compromise and sacrifice are the name of the game,
As your wife I am proud to carry your last name.
My heart is full of love, my eyes desire,
One kiss from you lights my body on fire.

We are building a foundation for everlasting love,
We are made for each other; we fit like a glove.
You are considerate of my feelings, and I am of yours,
You are a gentleman; you still open doors.

Sometimes it's the little things in love that really count,
I will accept all your love in no certain amount.
Just a simple hug to let me know you care,
If I need someone to talk to, you are always there.

We tell each other about how we really feel,
This love is no fantasy; this love is real.
Going out together is never an issue,
I'm proud to be by your side; I'm proud to be with you.

Our captivating love radiates through our smiles,
The twists and turns of this love journey go for miles and miles.
We are each other's best friends as well as lovers,
I can't see us ever loving any others.

Our love is not celebrated just once a year,
There is no guesswork; our feelings are clear.
We celebrate our love each and every day,
By the things we do, and by the things we say.

Looking for Love

I've searched high and low,
And still, I can't find love.
Is it behind the curtains?
Or under the sofa cushions?
Or maybe hiding in the back of the closet?
Where is this thing called love?
Why is it so far from my reach?
One time I thought I found it,
This strange thing called love.
But sadly, I lost it,
It slipped right out of my grip.
And then I thought I found it again,
But it was just an illusion.
Why is it so hard to find this thing called love?
Hey, there it goes again!
I found that slippery thing called love.
But wait, it's getting away from me!
I have to catch it before it leaves.
I searched so long for this thing called love,
So, I'm not letting it go this time.
I'm chasing behind it,
Going full-speed ahead.
We may crash in the end,
But at least I'll have love.
Just as I reach out to grasp it,
That sneaky fool disappears.
My heart sinks to my stomach,
And sadness overtakes me.

My heart yearns to be loved,
But love doesn't seem to want me.
What will it take for me to experience true love?
Or will I never find out?
There is a huge whole in my heart,
That I would like to be completely filled.
Not with sand or cement,
But with true, unconditional love.
Every time I think I've found it,
It takes me on a wild goose chase.
Why is love so hard to capture?
Why can't I find love?
It seems to be so easy for everyone else,
So why not for me?
My mother never loved me, and that makes me cry,
The man called my father could only show his love through abuse.
I thought friends loved me, but it was just false hope.
When he promised to love me, I thought I had finally found it,
But sadly, it was just a game.
Then I ventured out to find love again,
But I ended up right back where I started.
I've searched high and low,
And still, I can't find love.
Is it behind the curtains?
Or under the sofa cushions?
Or maybe hiding in the back of the closet?
Where is this thing called love?
Why is it so far from my reach?

Right Love Wrong Man

She gave him her whole heart,
But he tore it apart.
Shattered it to pieces,
The heart ache never eases.
Her tears of pain fall,
Because she gave him her all.
Late nights and lies,
His intentions a disguise.
Brought her to this place,
The betrayal so hard to erase.
Hoping that he would change,
But things remained the same.
Her love he took advantage,
Now leaving her so broken and damaged.
She thought they would be together,
Happy in love forever.
But that was all a silly dream,
A part of his whole scheme.
He loved no one,
He just played with her for fun.
Saying all the right things,
Playing with her heartstrings.
To get what he could get,
For this he has no regrets.
But now she's suffering,
Wounds of her heart uncovering.
Pain hurting her soul so bad,
The sorrow in her eyes was so sad.

But the signs were there,
Signs that he really didn't care.
But she wanted to believe,
Her heart he would never deceive.
She chose to ignore,
Because it would hurt her core.
To know that his love was false,
So, she accepted his faults.
By love, she was blinded,
Now she will constantly be reminded.
Of this aching heartbreak,
But how long will it take?
For her to move on,
From a love so wrong.
She will need time to heal,
And time to feel.
Whole and complete again,
Before she goes back in.
Into the next love situation,
Without a fixation.
On the last failed love episode,
Where love was not equally shown.
Things will not always be this way,
She will find that love one day.
And this pain will be forgotten,
Another disastrous love she won't be caught in.
She had the right love plan,
But sadly, it was just for the wrong man.

Self-Love Poem

In a world where chaos takes its toll,
Where shadows creep and hearts grow cold,
It's time to embrace a love so rare,
A love that starts within, a love so fair.

Write me a poem about self-love,
A verse that heals and rises above,
For in these lines, lay the power and strength,
To ignite our souls and go to great lengths.

Within ourselves, a light does glow,
A flame that burns, a seed to sow,
Nurture it with care, let it grow,
And watch as self-love begins to show.

It starts with acceptance, from deep within,
Knowing we're flawed, but embracing our skin,
For perfection is just a myth we chase,
But self-love brings solace, in its own grace.

Write me a poem about self-love,
A melody that sings of stars above,
Of dreams that shimmer and hopes that soar,
As we learn to love ourselves, more and more.

See, self-love is not selfish, it's a necessity,
A gentle reminder of our true divinity,
For when we love ourselves, we shine so bright,

Illuminating the world with pure delight.

So let the words dance upon the page,
Tell a tale of self-love, of turning the page,
For in these verses, lies a truth so grand,
A reminder that self-love is where we must stand.

Write me a poem about self-love,
A symphony of kindness, push, and shove,
Let it echo through the chambers of our heart,
And guide us on a journey, a fresh new start.

For self-love is a gift that we deserve,
To cherish and honor, with every nerve,
So, write me a poem, a love letter divine,
A reminder that self-love is yours and mine.

In every line, let love unfurl,
A blessing to embrace, a precious pearl,
For in self-love, we find our true worth,
A treasure that lasts, beyond this earthly turf.

So, poem of self-love, let your words be bold,
Inspire the weary, ignite the old,
In your verses, let love take flight,
And guide us home, to a love so bright.

Words of Fire

Your words engulf me in your angry flames,
Burn your hatred into my delicate skin.
Sear my heart with your unbearable heat,
Your words burn me to the 3rd degree.
My self-esteem melts with every degrading second,
Blazing are the words you throw my way.
The fire behind your eyes scorches my soul,
A combustion of still-healing permanent scars.
Peeling back my skin of embarrassment,
The excruciating pain brings me to my knees.
Your harsh resentment surrounds me like an inferno,
The bright glow of the flames lick at my spirit.
And at the end of your fiery tirade,
When the embers have finally cooled.
Is a calm smoky silence,
As your words evaporate into the air.
Leaving my heart on fire,
And my soul ablaze.

Piece of my Heart

Should I give it to him?
My heart?
My friendship?
Just a piece of my heart.

I have feelings for him,
But I am not sure.
Is he worthy?
Of a piece of my heart.

Will he love me truly?
Care like he says he does.
Will he appreciate?
A piece of my heart.

Are we meant to be?
Together forever?
Will he value?
A piece of my heart.

Love has hurt me before,
Will he do the same?
I'm just not sure,
If I should give him a piece of my heart.

So conflicted inside; I am,
Struggling with my fears.
Will I regret?
Giving him a piece of my heart.

Once I give him all the pieces,
It will make a whole.
A whole heart to cherish,
Made from all the pieces of my heart.

If Loving You Is Wrong

If loving you is wrong,
Then I am willing to pay the price,
Because what we have feels oh so right.
If loving you is wrong,
Why do I feel so alive?
And I get excited every time that you arrive.
If loving you is wrong,
If this kind of love is hard to find,
Then why are you constantly on my mind?
If loving you is wrong,
Then why am I glowing so bright?
My aura radiates through the dark night.
If loving you is wrong,
Why is it you I want to stand beside?
With love in my eyes and a sense of pride.
If loving you is wrong,
And I want to be your wife,
Grant me this one wish for the rest of my life.
If loving you is wrong,
Then I don't wanna be right,
Because I need a love like yours in my life.
So, loving you isn't wrong,
That we can't deny,
No matter how we try.
Loving you isn't wrong,
And we know exactly why,
It's that sparkle you have for me in your eye.

Broken Promises

Yes, you know what they are,
Promises, which are meant to be broken.
Those crossed fingers,
And hopes to die,
Unfortunately, won't be kept.
Those solemnly swear promises,
Hand on the heart,
The pinky swears and right hand on the bible,
They will be broken.
Those I would never lie to you,
Or you have to believe me,
Won't mean a thing; really.
These promises will be dismissed,
By lies and betrayals,
And half-truths and poor excuses.
Those words of honor,
Will be spoken from the lips,
Of someone who won't really mean them.
And you will be let down.
Your heart will be heavy with disappointment,
Because they didn't keep their word.
The crossing of their heart,
Was supposed to solidify their vow,
But instead, you got broken promises.
Actions speak louder than words,
We all know the saying.
Sometimes it's not intentional,
Other times it's deliberate.
But promises were made to be broken,
And the majority of the time they are.

Fourteen Verses of Love

1 sunny day you came into my life,

2 years later, I'm proud to be your wife.

3 beautiful children who look just like you,

4 ever grateful I said I do.

5 is the number that makes our family complete,

6 dozen roses from you are a special treat.

7 of your sweet kisses sets me on fire,

8 more kisses take me higher and higher.

9 scented candles to set the mood right,

10 love songs crooning as we dance tonight.

11 million reasons why I'm here to stay,

12 strikes midnight, and we celebrate another day.

13 more years and beyond I plan to spend with you,

14 verses of love just to say I love you.

I'll Wait

I'll wait until you come my way,
My true love that was meant for me.
When we find each other, our love will stay,
With each other together for eternity.

I'm in no rush to find out what's out there,
Because the one meant for me, he will know.
That all he needs is right here,
Just waiting to tell him so.

We will know that it is true love,
Because the way we feel will make it clear.
It will be blessed from the heavens above,
Because God will always be near.

Both our hearts intertwined together,
Will be the center of our life.
Love, loyalty, and trust forever,
You will find in me your wife.

We will always make it through,
All the stormy nights and rocky roads.
Because you love me, and I love you,
And we know how this love thing goes.

*Things won't always be perfect,
But we will stand together strong.
Because in the end we know our love is worth it,
Even when things are going wrong.*

*We will always cherish the love we have,
And never let anyone come between.
Because we are blessed with what we have,
You're my king, and I'm your queen.*

*Our beautiful unity, our wonderful partnership,
Will reign like an empire.
This beautiful, wonderful courtship,
Will hopefully inspire.*

*I will adore you, and you will adore me,
Our love radiating through.
Loving each other unconditionally and faithfully,
As true lovers should do.*

*So, I'll wait patiently for you,
Until it's our turn for love; in due time.
For things to fall into place the way they do,
Then I will be yours, and you will be mine.*

The Love of a Comforter

In the stillness of my soul, a whisper I hear,
A gentle beckoning, drawing me near,
A love so divine, cascading from above,
I feel it in my bones, God's eternal love.

Like a rushing river, it sweeps me away,
Carrying me to realms where worries can't sway,
In its current, I'm embraced by divine grace,
The burdens I carried; I now release.

As each tear falls, like droplets on a leaf,
The pain I once held begins to find relief,
Transformed within, as the sun breaks through,
I'm bathed in a love that makes me brand-new.

Like a phoenix rising, reborn from the flame,
I shed my old self, let go of all the blame,
For in God's love, I find my purest worth,
A love that accepts me, flaws, and all on this earth.

In the depths of despair, I was lost and afraid,
But God's love reached out, showed me a new way,
I dance on the strings of forgiveness and grace,
Wrapped in His love, a warm and gentle embrace.

The storms of life may rage, the darkness may loom,
But in accepting God's love, I conquer the gloom,
For His love is the anchor when troubles arise,
A beacon of hope, guiding me through life's cries.

Like a lighthouse in the storm, it guides me home,
To a place of peace, where my spirit can roam,
In God's love, I find solace and serenity,
A sanctuary where I am truly set free.

And as I walk this path, hand in hand with my Maker,
I am filled with a love that shines brighter and greater,
Accepting God's love has transformed who I am,
A vessel of love, arms open wide like a lamb.

So, let us embrace this divine love so pure,
Let it heal our wounds, as its power endures,
For in accepting God's love, we find our truest selves,
And bask in a love that forever compels.

Future Love

I see us always together,
Making future plans to be,
Together in love forever.
I haven't met you yet,
But I know you are near,
The paths of our lives are already set.
To love each other endlessly,
This is what we plan to do,
Fulfilling the desires of our hearts tremendously.
Anxiously I can't wait for us to see,
What the world has in store,
For the heart-stopping love between you and me.
Darling, have no fear,
We will get through the turbulent storms,
I see our future... and it's clear.
I promise to love and cherish you,
Until I have no more breath in me,
This solemn oath I take is true.
This love is what I pray for,
And what I seriously want,
Is for our unbreakable future love to soar.
Our hearts beating like busy swarms,
The desires for each other in our eyes,
This love taking shape in many forms.
Designing our life so artfully,
Making hearts fly high,
I want this love for eternity.

Clear Bruises

They aren't easily visible, but they are there,
Covering her body.
Every space was taken over,
You're just not aware.
No, it isn't darkened skin or blackened eyes,
Broken bones.
Or permanent scars,
But they're hidden deep inside.
A broken spirit,
With no direction.
Dreams long lost,
The pain she has to deal with.
Hope long gone,
Days of happiness exist no more.
Peace is a foreign word,
The false smile she puts on.
It's not your typical,
Not easily noticed.
To you, she looks normal,
But it's emotional and mental.
It's just as bad,
Sometimes even worse.
Bruised is her heart,
The look in her eyes so sad.
Sorrow fills her being,
Her unheard cries in the night.

Torturing her soul,
Don't be fooled by what the eyes aren't seeing.
Burdened by inner pain,
Hollowed from the inside out.
A shell of her former self,
Her tears fall like rain.
She's calling out,
Looking for an escape.
A way to recover herself,
To figure out what love's all about.
Why is she so trapped?
A windowless room,
A doorless house,
The energy to continue to fight sapped,
Broken and shattered to pieces,
Too many to put back together.
Love has lost,
As her zest for life decreases.
You may not be able to see that they are there,
They are so well hidden.
They have left their mark,
Even though her bruises are clear.

Embrace Self

In the depths of my soul, I seek self-love,
A sacred voyage into the wilderness of my being,
Where shadows dance with light, and vulnerability blossoms.

I am a tapestry of brilliance and blunders,
A symphony of hues cascading through existence.
My flaws, like cracks upon a porcelain vase,
Are the very essence of my humanity.

So let us unravel the complexities of self-acceptance,
And cherish the mosaic of ups and downs,
Each stitch a testament to resilience and growth.

See, I am not a diamond without blemish,
But a constellation of scars illuminated by moonlight.
My imperfections are the constellations in a night sky,
Guiding me towards self-discovery and inner freedom.

Like a river, I flow through valleys and mountains,
Winding and meandering between triumphs and failures.
Each bend reveals hidden gems, lessons learned,
And a love that transcends conventional boundaries.

Look closer, dear reader, and you shall see,
A forest within me, where strength takes root,
And compassion blooms amidst the thorns.

For self-love is the fragrance of wildflowers,
The touch of the sun's caress on winter skin.
It is the universe' way of whispering truths,
And igniting sparks of courage within our hearts.

Embrace your quirks, your idiosyncrasies,
For they are the brushstrokes on the canvas of your soul.
You are a work of art, unfinished and evolving,
A masterpiece in constant transformation.

Within your flaws lies unimaginable beauty,
A kaleidoscope of strengths waiting to unfold.
Do not fear the shadows, for they are your guides,
Leading you towards the radiance within.

So, dance with your vulnerabilities,
Embrace them like old friends with stories to tell.
For they teach you the art of self-compassion,
And nurture the seeds of growth within.

Let self-love be your compass, your sanctuary,
A refuge in moments of doubt and uncertainty.

In this journey of self-discovery, embrace all that you are,
For your flaws and strengths are what make you uniquely you.

In the vast expanse of this world, find solace within yourself,
And know that you are worthy of love, within and without.
For self-love is the ultimate act of defiance,
A rebellion against a world that often tells us otherwise.

So, dear reader, take this poem as an invitation,
To unravel the depths of your own being,
To embrace the multifaceted nature of self-acceptance,
And awaken the dormant love within your soul.

For in this act of self-love, liberation awaits,
And you shall soar, untethered, into the realm of authenticity.
Discover your own wildest hues, your hidden strengths,
And let the symphony of your existence resound.

Whirlwind

We're caught up in a whirlwind romance,
A dance of love; oh, what a lovely dance.
We're caught up in a whirlwind romance,
The feelings you ignite in me keep me in a trance.
We're caught up in a whirlwind romance,
I'm glad I gave this love thing another chance.
We're caught up in a whirlwind romance,
This love is well-traveled from the mountains of the Himalayas to the towers of France.
We're caught up in a whirlwind romance,
My life was already meaningful, but your tender love made it enhance.
We're caught up in a whirlwind romance,
Our meeting each other didn't happen by happenstance.
We're caught up in a whirlwind romance,
I couldn't have known a love like this existed in advance.
We're caught up in a whirlwind romance,
This wonderful, beautiful heart-entwining love is our romance.

Loving You

In the secret chambers of the soul's design,
Amidst the echoes of silence and fleet thoughts,
There resides a love, profound and divine,
A love that transcends all earthly knots.

It blooms within, like a wildflower rare,
Nurtured by thy gentle touch of grace,
Unfurling petals, vibrant and fair,
A kaleidoscope of colors, a sacred embrace.

For self-love is the key to transformation,
A power infinite, yet often overlooked,
To nurture the roots of self-dedication,
And witness our spirits rise, reborn and hooked.

Within its depths lies resilience untold,
A wellspring of strength, like the mighty oak,
Though buffeted by tempests, it holds,
With unwavering faith, refusing to choke.

It whispers amidst the chaos and din,
A soothing balm to wounds that cannot heal,
Mending fragments of our tattered skin,
Infusing our souls with a love that's real.

It paints the world with hues so bright,
Transforming shadows to ethereal light,
Embracing every flaw, every fight,
And adorning our spirits, feathers in flight.

For in self-love's embrace, we find the key,
To mental well-being, a tapestry of peace,
A sanctuary where minds wander free,
And anxieties in their chains release.

It conquers the fear of vulnerability,
Unshackling hearts, a freedom profound,
And in nurturing self, forms a unity,
That radiates love, spreading warmth around.

Embrace thyself, both the dusk and dawn,
With all thy beauty, thy flaws interlaced,
For self-love is an art to be practiced, drawn,
A masterpiece of self-discovery and grace.

So let us dance to the rhythm of our hearts,
In sync with the song of self-acceptance,
With every step, shedding the world's dark arts,
And embracing our uniqueness, and our existence.

For in self-love's symphony, we are complete,
A chorus that sings, resonating within,
With hearts healed and souls replete,
We find true fulfillment, where echoes begin.

No Boundaries

In the realm where hardships dwell,
A single mother's story I must tell,
With unwavering love, her heart swells,
As she embraces the challenges that fell.

Through thickets of despair, she weaves,
A tapestry of resilience she retrieves,
With every stride, she never grieves,
For her child's dreams, her spirit cleaves.

In the face of storms, her spirit dauntless,
She stands tall, unyielding, never relentless,
A beacon of hope, forever ageless,
The world may falter, but her love remains boundless.

Like a solitary tree in the vast wilderness,
Her sacrifice blooms with internal finesse,
For a child she adores, she undoubtedly professes,
To paint their world in shades of happiness.

Amidst the darkness, her light does glow,
A nurturing presence, a shelter bestowed,
Her soothing whispers, like a love song's flow,
Guide her child through shadows, fearsome and low.

With arms of strength, she carries the burden,
Her child cradled gently, never a word muffled,

Through sleepless nights, her love earns,
A symphony of lullabies woven never troubled.

In her embrace, time slows its pace,
Creating a sanctuary, a sacred space,
Her kisses, like petals, softly trace,
The contours of a child's blossoming face.

She is the river, steady and strong,
Sculpting a path where dreams belong,
With every ripple, she pushes along,
Empowering her child to grow, to belong.

Her touch, like warm sunlight's caress,
Melts away sorrow, leaves no distress,
She stitches broken dreams, no-less,
Crafting hope into an ethereal dress.

And in her child's eyes, a reflection true,
Of unwavering love, both old and new,
A testament to her devotion, to all she'd pursue,
Through thorns and fires, she'd forever ensue.

So let admiration flow, like rivers deep,
For a single mother's love, forever to keep,
For in her embrace, the heart finds its peace,
A love immortal, a bond that will never cease.

A Forgiving Love

In shadows deep, were sorrows dwell as night,
A sinner's soul, stained by the weight of sin,
An ancient dance of wrongs, a blurred sight,
Within my heart, the chaos swells within.

Yet through this darkness, where demons reside,
Where guilt's sharp blade, cuts deep into my skin,
A light divine, within my heart abides,
Unyielding love forgives the path I've been.

Like a gentle rain on a parched plain,
Your tender grace quenches my weary soul,
Pulling me up from the depths of deepest pain,
Your forgiveness makes me once again whole.

With celestial brush, you paint my bleak sky,
Colors of hope on canvas stained with strife,
Whispering secrets, answering my cry,
In love's embrace, you breathe eternal life.

Oh, boundless love, that knows no limit nor end,
A river of mercy, deep and vast as the sea,
Your grace o'erflows, my broken heart to mend,
Redemption's tide, my spirit is set free.

Through thorny paths and valleys of despair,
You never falter, never cease to guide,
Your hand extended, reaching out in care,
With open arms, you stand close by my side.

Like the sun's warm rays on a winter's morn,
Your love's embrace, thaws my frozen heart,
Transforming darkness into golden dawn,
In grace and mercy, I am set apart.

Oh, sinner's soul, wrapped within divine grace,
You're but a spark within a fire of love,
Struggle no more, for in God's warm embrace,
Forgiveness flows from heaven's throne above.

Though we stumble and fall down on this earth,
In God's love, we find strength to rise above,
For in His heart, we find our souls' true worth,
Embraced by endless mercy and boundless love.

So let us all, with grateful hearts, declare,
The wondrous love that sets our spirits free,
For in His arms, we find solace and care,
In God's embrace, we find eternity.

About the Author

Blaque Diamond is a totally blind author, poet, motivational speaker, songwriter, and entrepreneur residing in Greensboro, North Carolina. She was born in Charlotte, North Carolina, but left when she was eleven months old and grew up in Charleston, South Carolina. She spent her childhood engrossed in books. Instead of playing outside with the other children, she could be found with her head buried in books. It was no surprise that she developed a love for writing. She started writing when she was eleven years old, due to urging from her 5th-grade teacher, who saw something in her that she didn't see in herself. She started writing poetry and children's stories, which started as a hobby, but began to reflect things in her life that she was going through. The more she wrote, the more writing became like therapy to get her through the toughest years of her life.

Blaque Diamond began publishing her work in 2017, and has published 12 books in counting. Her genres include children's literature, poetry, romance, contemporary African-American fiction, erotica, and more. Blaque Diamond has also co-authored 4 titles along with other talented authors under the genre of non-fiction.

When she is not working on her next publication, Blaque Diamond enjoys traveling, shopping, listening to music, binge watching true crime shows, whipping up her next batch of natural skin care products, and spending time with her loved ones.

Keep in Contact

If you would like to follow the author on social media, visit these links:

Https://www.youtube.com/writerblaquediamond
Https://www.instagram.com/writerblaquediamond
Https://www.facebook.com/writerblaquediamond
Https://www.tiktok.com/writerblaquediamond

Other Books by Blaque Diamond

<u>Words of My Heart</u>

<u>His or Her Betrayal?</u>

<u>Love, Lies, and Heartbreak Vol. 1</u>

<u>What You Won't Do</u>

<u>Dream Paramour</u>

<u>It's Our Anniversary</u>

www.ingramcontent.com/pod-product-compliance
Lightning Source LLC
Chambersburg PA
CBHW011550070526
44585CB00023B/2535